Barb

Very best wishes from

Richard

aka 'The Great Simmoni'

TOP QUALITY
ONE-LINERS

TOP QUALITY ONE-LINERS

'Stage Comedy Material at its Best!'
for Amateur and Professionals
Comedians.

RICHARD SIMMONS
aka 'The Great Simmoni'

ISBN: 978-1-0686829-1-9

Cover Design
Elisabeth Heissler Design
www.ehgraphicdesign.co.uk

Interior Design and Typesetting
Elisabeth Heissler Design
www.ehgraphicdesign.co.uk

Dedicated to my daughter Emma,
in her 20 year losing battle with M.E.

Contents

No content with bad language

Introduction

Please read to understand the connection to Youtube.com

Throughout my life I have always taken a delight in a good joke. In my view jokes do not have to be offensive. A good joke often has a really clever construction to it that is a beauty to behold. You only need to buy a typical book of "5000 Funny Jokes" to realise how tedious and 'unfunny' so many so-called jokes can be. The books may be two inches thick but nobody in their right mind wants to wade through a load of rubbish simply to enjoy the odd decent one.

An example of a classic very cleverly constructed joke was written by the great Bob Monkhouse:
"When I said I was going to be a Comedian they all laughed... they're not laughing anymore!"

My own introduction into comedy was as follows.... The Golf Club in Kenilworth, Warwickshire for many years put on an annual revue by the members, comprising singers and a few light hearted sketches. Always short of acts, I was persuaded do some stage Magic, initially based upon tricks I had performed for the grandkids at Christmas. As my confidence grew, the magic got pretty eccentric and not a little dangerous! The magic was well received by the audience and became an annual favourite at the Christmas Show.

Gaining great confidence from the 'Magic' turns, one year I felt sufficiently emboldened to try some 'Stand Up Comedy'; doing Magic in the first half of the show and Comedy in the second half. Initially the comedy was fairly mediocre as nerves caused jokes to be delivered too fast and punchlines at times were missed. The audience was always kind and genuinely encouraging however. Of course they love it when it goes wrong anyway!

After a few years I was getting plenty of laughs out of the audience, and at times 'had them in the palm of my hand'! I found short one-liners were far more liked, and a much safer bet than long complicated jokes. Obviously with one-liners **timing is everything**.

Not all jokes read well 'off the page'. If some seem a little 'dry' then you might try to imagine saying them on the stage in a 'dead-pan' tone. Looking at great pros on Youtube.com like Mick Miller might establish the exact dead-pan tone that I would suggest you seek.

Many of the modern comedians choose to do 'observational comedy' but that is not a style I have tried, preferring 'out and out joke telling'.

If the person reading this book is a complete beginner at 'Stand up' then I strongly urge you to take the plunge and have a go. With so many really poor comedians out there, the bar is set pretty low and the worst that can happen is a few boos... **trust me on this, they will not boo the jokes in this book!**

A word about the Audience...at the Golf Club shows we always did a Friday and Saturday evening. It was staggering how much the audience varied. At times we could land a cracker of a show on the Friday with audience clearly loving it all; on the Saturday the same material and jokes could fall flat and we would be wading in treacle trying to get off the stage! It happens and you just have to take it on the chin. If it happens all the time though...then it's you, not them!

My Comedy and Magic can be viewed on YouTube.com at: 'Simmo's Comedy and Magic Channel.'

https://www.youtube.com/@simmoscomedyandmagicchanne6734

The jokes in the early pages of the book are set out in the exact sequence that I told them at the various shows. This gives the reader the chance to see my own interpretation of how the joke might be delivered.
Simply scan the QR Code on the pages to see the live performance of the jokes on the page.

I honestly believe that I have a talent for writing or spotting a good joke. In this book I am going to be bold enough to say these are all **quality one-liners** and a few really funny longer jokes too. They are particularly suitable for telling in public at parties, weddings, on stage etc. My view is the jokes are good enough for the novice, amateur comedian and even the pro may wish to grab a few!

None of the jokes are intended to be offensive. They are told in the same spirit of say the late Les Dawson. The more he joked about the wife and mother-in-law, the more we knew he really loved them. We cannot ruin the humour of life by keeping everything so politically correct and sterile that we die of boredom...

ENJOY...

Random 365

In this section we have listed all 365 One-Liners in random order. Many of the one-liners can be heard 'live' by scanning the QR code link shown on the pages:

1 **The wife says I ruined her birthday...... I said, "Don't be so absurd, I didn't even know it was your birthday."**

2 **I was driving along and I smashed into a magician. It wasn't my fault, he came out of nowhere.**

3 **I don't do many innuendos but I do slip one in occasionally.**

4 **How many optometrists does it take to change a light bulb? ......one or two..........one or two.......**

5 **I used to work for the Samaritans, but every time you call in sick they try to talk you out of it.**

6 **I phoned the incontinence hotline last night..... and all you get is a voice saying, "Can you hold please?"**

7 **A dog walker was found dead in the local park; the police have found the dog but they haven't got a lead.**

8 **Someone threw a bottle of omega 3 at me and hit me in the face. The doctor said, "Luckily you've only got super-fish-oil injuries."**

9 **I had to take the batteries out of my carbon monoxide detector; the constant beeping was making me nauseous.**

10 **In Egypt, archaeologists have found a mummy covered in nuts and chocolate chips........they think they have found the original Pharaoh Rocher.**

11 **I was at the ice cream van. I said, "I want to buy an ice cream please". He said, "Hundreds and thousands." I said, "We'll start with one and see how we go."**

12 **Bloke was found on the floor of his ice cream van covered in nuts and sprinkles........police think he topped himself.**

13 **Doctor Doctor, I get heartburn every time I eat birthday cake. "Well take the candles off next time."**

14 **It's the anniversary today of when the boomerang was invented........many happy returns.**

15 **I'm really annoyed. The local Neighbourhood Watch group had a meeting last night about some creepy weirdo in the area and I wasn't invited.**

16 **Police called at the house and said, "We have reason to believe that on August 15th you skateboarded down Kenilworth high street, naked, with a firework up your backside singing The Laughing Policeman. What do you have to say?" I said, "What was that date again?"**

17 **A guy knocked on my door and asked for a donation towards the new local swimming pool. I gave him a glass of water.**

18 **Viagra is now available in powdered form to put in your coffee. It doesn't help your sex life but it stops your biscuits going soft.**

19 **My mate Gav had terrible indigestion and he's died of an overdose of heartburn tablets. I can't believe that Gav-is-gone.**

20 **The wife's bisexual......what I really mean is she only does it twice a year.**

21 **To liven things up I've changed the bed for a trampoline .....last night the wife hit the roof.**

22 **The wife says to spice things up let's each pick a fantasy partner.....you know..... she says, "Mine's George Clooney, who's yours?"......Well, when I said, 'The babysitter' all hell broke loose.**

23 **The wife says, "You never tell me how much you love me." I said, "I know, I don't want to upset you."**

24 **The wife swallowed a load of scrabble tiles; she's in hospital because the doctor says if she goes to the toilet it could spell disaster.**

25 **A lorry carrying a big delivery of Vicks nasal spray has turned over on the M6..... police are warning motorists to expect no congestion for at least 8 hours.**

VIDEO 1

Jokes 1 to 25 can all be viewed at this Video Link.

I found the intro quite good by saying "before I tell you any jokes, I'm going to tell you a bit about my day". I then tell them the joke about missing my wife's Birthday, "I didn't even know it was her Birthday"; and one about me crashing my car into the Magicians on the way to the venue "he just appeared from nowhere"! The effect of this intro seemed to immediately establish a great rapport with the audience for the whole act.

This show is just one act in a full Christmas Pantomime. On the video it's useful to see that the choir are genuinely enjoying the jokes even though they have heard then before in rehearsals. →

→ Having established a 'knock about' atmosphere with the audience then messing up a few punchlines seems to cause as good a laugh as the correct punchlines. The joke "having discovered the original Pharoah Roche' "is a classic example where a good and fairly simple joke can go wrong if you let your concentration slip.

I decide to leave the stage and re-enter with some 'late traffic news:'

"A lorry load of Vicks Nasal Spray has overturned on the M6.... Police report that they are not expecting any congestion for the next 8 hours"!

In summary though, a great audience.

26 **When I met the wife she said she didn't believe in sex before marriage...I should have checked she believed in it after marriage.**

27 **I always know when the wife's up...... I can hear her scraping the toast.**

28 **I tried that internet dating, but I soon realised it wasn't for me when they matched me up with the wife.**

29 **The wife was really flattered when they named a rose after her, mind you she wasn't too pleased when she read the description in the catalogue....'not much good in a bed, but fine up against a wall'.**

30 **I knew her mother was coming round when I saw the canary throw itself in the cat's mouth.**

31 **We get a lot of these militant feminists these days, I take my hat off to them....they don't like that.**

32 **I went to bed with a blind girl last night, she said I had the biggest whatsit she'd ever laid her hands on .... I said, "You're pulling my leg."**

33 **You don't appreciate a lot of stuff in school until you get older. Little things like being spanked by a middle-aged woman everyday....... things you'd pay good money for in later life.**

34 **I saw the doctor, he said, "You've only got 10 to live." I said, "10 what.....years, months, days??"....He said, " 9. 8. 7. ...."**

35 **An Englishman, Scotsman and Irishman go into a pub...... the landlord says, "Is this some kind of joke?"**

36 **I still remember that Beatles song like it was yesterday.**

37 **The only benefit from studying algebra is that it helped us when our children needed help with their algebra.**

38 **My mate keeps drinking brake fluid, but he says he's not addicted......he can stop when he wants.**

39 **I hear there's a new Hollywood blockbuster called 'Constipated'............it hasn't come out yet.**

40 **I went to see a psychic yesterday, he said, "What's your name?"..... I said, "I want my money back."**

41 **Deep down, I knew that scuba diving wasn't for me.**

42 **A woman walks into a bar and asks for a 'double entendre' ....so the barman gives her one.**

43 **My blinking neighbour was banging on my door at 3 o'clock this morning....lucky I was still up playing the drums.**

44 **My mate had an accident and fell in an upholstery machine, but fortunately he's completely recovered.**

45 **That eBay's good, I sold my homing pigeon 8 times last month.**

46 **I've just been done for my part in a timeshare fraud, luckily I only have to go to prison two weeks every year.**

47 **I want congratulate the Viagra Pharmaceutical Company, they had record sales of 2 million tablets last month......well done lads, keep it up.**

48 **A girl lying in the sun on a park bench. A tramp says, "eh luv, what about the two of us getting it on?" Horrified she says, "What sort of girl do you think I am? I'm not one of your cheap pick-ups." The tramp says, "Well you're already lying in my bed."**

49 **I said to the wife "I'll try not to be condescending; that means I won't talk down to you."**

50 **My dad was a roofer. He's not with us anymore. So Dad.....if you're up there......** **(MICK MILLER)**

VIDEO 2

Jokes 26 to 50 can all be viewed at this Video Link.

Not the easiest audience hence delivery of jokes speeds up. (It's so much easier to get a nice slow rhythm when the audience is easy.)

It was at the time Boris was getting elected and I tried to go off script to start with by trying to get current and topical. Hence a rather slow start but recovered the audience a little further along. Lesson learnt, 'try to get too clever at your peril; get audience and confidence going first before straying off script'.

51 **My dad had a weird hobby; collecting empty bottles; which sounds much better than saying he was an alcoholic.** (MICK MILLER)

52 **My dad knew when he was going to die.........the judge told him.** (MICK MILLER)

53 **My dad was sentenced to the electric chair. Anniversaries are difficult....we just put a wreath by the plug socket.** (MICK MILLER)

54 **My Dad died eating a bowl of Cheerios..... choked on one......we never got the chance to say goodbye.** (MICK MILLER)

55 **The wife said, "If you were half a man you would take the kids to the circus." I said, "If I was half a man, I'd be in the circus."** (MICK MILLER)

56 **I was in the circus for many years; well I say 'in the circus'; I was the only one who could get the tent back in the bag.** (MICK MILLER)

57 **I was a human cannon ball for a while but the pay's crap......... sixty quid a week plus a bit of mileage.** (MICK MILLER)

58 **The contortionist at the circus has died suddenly................he died in his own arms.** (MICK MILLER)

59 **My background is very much in the circus.........I came from a long line of conga dancers.**

60 **My brother had a great act on stilts....... I always looked up to him.**

61 **The wife's got a new job, but it's not easy to say what it is.....she sells seashells on the sea shore.**

62 **I bought the wife a new fridge for her birthday. She wasn't pleased....... but her face lit up when she opened the door.**

63 **Wife came home, just back from the beauty parlour. I said, "What's wrong, was it closed?"**

64 **I say to the wife I love you just the way you are, but she never listens, she just goes on putting weight on.**

65 **The wife said, "Will you stop walking round the house singing I'm a believer". I didn't know what she was on about....then I saw her face.**

66 **The wife came home and caught me wearing her best dress....I said, "Don't leave me, I can change."**

67 **The wife left me, she says I think more about football than her....I was gutted, I've been with that girl for 5 seasons.**

68 **Two cannibals eating a clown. One says to the other "Does he taste funny to you?"**

69 **Two cannibals eating meal. One says to the other, "Your wife makes a lovely meal." The other says, "Yes, I'm going to miss her."**

VIDEO 3

Jokes 51 to 69 can all be viewed at this Video Link.

You will notice I have a music stand to my side with a crib sheet of the keyword to give me the next joke. I agree it's not very professional but there again, I am not a professional (!), I am only performing very rarely and for no fee. Having the sheet available to view gives a warm feeling that it limits how far wrong things can go. The audience no doubt notices but seems not bothered by this approach. With a show of one-liners, a rhythm becomes established whereby there is time to 'glance for the next joke' whilst they are laughing at the previous joke. I fully accept it would be a 'no-no' in a professional scenario.

This show was a very easy audience and again the choir are enjoying the banter. The "I'll try not to be condescending....... that means talking down to you Lorraine!" is a great line for getting the audience on side.

One of my favourite jokes in this show viz "......my father choked to death on a Cheerio.... (pause). We never got the chance to say goodbye". →

→ I tend to run a few jokes in from the same category, for example three or four circus jokes, then some cannibal jokes, then some wife jokes.

The show ends with three fairly long jokes which I feel are all very strong:

A butcher is doing really badly but notices the Antique shops in the area doing well. He changes his shop to an antique shop and gets a Leg of Lamb out of the freezer and puts it in the window with a note saying "Lord Nelson's Hip, £200". A customer comes in, explaining he is a collector of memorabilia and offers £180 which the butcher gleefully accepts.

The Butcher gets a Sheep's Brain out of the freezer and puts it in the window "Sir Francis Drake's Brain, £150."

The same customer returns and offers £140 which the butcher takes.

The Butcher now puts two small potatoes in the window just as the customer is passing by. Getting a little suspicious the customer says "you're not going to tell me they are Lord Nelson's testicles, are you?"

"No, they're King Edwards! "replies the Butcher............ boom, boom! (King Edwards Potatoes)

An Irishman in a pub finds a Genie in a bottle. The Genie says you are so lucky to find me you can have any two wishes.......→

→ The Irishman has a good long think and says " oil' ave a never-ending pint of Guinness please". He's has a good long drink then the Genie says " What is your second request?" After more deliberation the Irishman says "I 'tink 'oil 'ave another of them please."

The Mother-in-law went missing and drowned at sea. The Coast Guard rang me in the early hours. He says Mr Simmons I have terrible news, we have found your Mother-in-law washed up on the shore drowned. "Oh, that's terrible" I said. "But it's not that simple Sir" said the Coast Guard, "she's completely naked and she's got 6 prize lobsters hooked onto the corpse. We don't know what to do for the best?". So I said "well how about you have 3, we'll have 3, and we'll set her on the next tide!"

70 **Did you hear about the cannibal in a restaurant.....he ordered the waiter!**

71 **Doctor, I keep thinking that I'm a bell. "Well take these and if it doesn't clear up give me a ring."**

72 **Doctor, I keep seeing fish. Have you seen an optician? "No," I said, "I keep seeing fish, not opticians!"**

73 **Doctor I keep sleep walking. Well go home, take these and sprinkle them on the floor. Are they tablets to make me sleep? No, they're tin tacks!**

74 **Doctor I think I'm a moth. Why are you seeing me not a psychiatrist? Well your light was on.**

75 **Teacher says to Jonny "Give me two pronouns." Jonny says, " What, me"?**

76 **A friend of ours has just lost his job as an archaeologist......to be honest his job was in ruins anyway.**

77 **My wife gave me a book on Feng Shui.......I didn't know where to put it.**

78 **I bought my wife a rug of eBay. It said mint condition. When I got it, there was a hole in the middle.**

79 **My wife says every time our neighbour sees his wife he kisses her. "Why can't you do that?" I said, "I hardly know her."**

80 **I said to my wife "Do you really need to iron that bra, there's not that much to put in it?" She replied, "I iron your boxer shorts don't I?"**

81 **We've got a new dog called Rolex. He's a watch dog.**

82 **Father-and-son cannibals are in the jungle. Suddenly they spot a beautiful girl. The son says, "Dad let's eat her." The father replies, "No, let's take her home and eat your mother!"**

83 **A sign outside a pet shop 'Dead canary for sale - not going cheap'.**

84 **Two parrots sitting on a perch, one says to the other, "Can you smell fish?"**

VIDEO 4

Jokes 70 to 84 can all be viewed at this Video Link.

Not a bad show. The audience loves it when the "Doctor I keep thinking I'm a bell" joke ends with the wrong punchline. It's uncanny how a mistake can liven the whole act up, helping the bond with the audience.

A couple of jokes to round off the performance:

A priest goes into the Confessional. The Priest finding the silence a bit odd, decided to tap on the wall. The tramp says "It's no good tapping on the wall mate, there's no paper in here either!"

A woman goes to the doctors and says "Doctor my husband snores, and sleeps with his mouth open. We live in the country and last night a mouse has gone straight down his throat. What can we do?" →

→ The Doctor says "well this is not really a medical matter, we don't really cover this sort of thing, but my advice would be to get a piece of string and a hook and lower a piece of cheese into his mouth."

She says "Ok, I'll go down to the market and get a couple of Fish Heads." (pause)

"Fish Heads" says the Doctor, "What do you want Fish Heads for?"

"Well we've got to get the cat out first!" she says.

85 **Apple is merging with Blackberry; they're bringing out a new electronic device....it's called The Crumble.**

86 **When the phone goes "Do you want to change your energy supplier?", I find the best reply is, "No, I'm quite happy with food."**

87 **A man walked in to the doctor's with a lettuce leaf sticking out of his ear. The doctor says, "That's strange." The man said, "That's just the tip of the iceberg."**

88 **I went to the doctor for a check-up. He said, "Have you had sex in the last 7 days?" I said, "Doctor, my birthday's in July...."**

89 **Doctor I think I'm suffering from low self-esteem. He said, "Don't worry too much, it's very common amongst total losers".**

90 **I said, Doctor I keep having this urge to paint myself gold. He said it was a guilt complex.**

91 **Doctor Doctor I keep seeing images of Donald Duck and Mickey Mouse. How long have you been having these Disney spells?**

92 **An old lady goes to the doctor's and says, "Doctor I keep doing these silent farts." The doctor says, "Well when is this happening?" The old lady says, "All the time Doctor, I've just done a silent fart right now". The doctor says, "Right, first we're going to get you a new hearing aid."**

93 **The wife was feeling unwell so I phoned the doctor for advice. He said, "Is she hot?" I said, "Well with a little make-up, and a short skirt...."**

94 **She says I'm full of my own importance.....anyway that's enough about her...**

95 **The wife said she keeps getting emails offering her cans of processed meat. I said, "It's only spam."**

96 **I ordered some bubble wrap just to see what it got delivered in.**

97 **I went on a website about toasters but there were too many pop-ups.**

98 **Me and the wife always hold hands. Well I say that........ if I let her go, she goes shopping.**

99 **I was shopping with the wife the other day. She went into a dress shop so I popped into the bookies just to kill a bit of time. A bloke comes up to me and says, "Do you want the winner of the 4.30 at Uttoxeter?" I said, "To be honest mate I've only got a small back garden."**

100 **Why did my wife cross the road? To go back into the first shoe shop we went in 3 hours ago.**

101 **Two tigers walking down the aisle of a supermarket. One says to the other, "Do you think it's quiet in here today?"**

102 **The staff at our supermarket are so slow I started using the self-checkout service ....I was named 'employee of the month'.**

103 **You've heard of 'Wash and Go' shampoo. There's a new one out now for down and outs, it's called 'Go and Wash'.**

104 **I went up to this guy selling The Big Issue the other day. I said, "Knock, knock", he said, "Who's there?" I said, "I thought you were supposed to be homeless?"**

105 **I'm doing my bit to help the homeless this Christmas, I've got stacks of cardboard boxes to give away.**

106 **I got sacked from my job in the Salvation Army soup kitchen- all I said was, "Hurry up you lot, some of us have got homes to go to!"**

107 **My friend's wife left him last week. He said she was going out for a bottle of milk and never came back. I said, "How are you coping?" "Not too bad" he said, "I'm getting by on the powdered stuff."**

108 **The wife dated a clown before we met....so I had some pretty big shoes to fill.**

109 **The wife comes from a long line of conga dancers.**

110 **I should have known it was a mistake to get married.... after I said, "I do", the vicar looked at her then turned to me and said, "Is that your final answer?"**

111 **I told the wife she'd drawn her eyebrows on too high... she looked surprised.**

112 **Every night the wife puts that mudpack on her face and slices of cucumber on her eyes. It doesn't work though, I can still tell it's her.**

113 **The wife sent me shopping today. She said, "Buy something to make me look sexy."....so I came back with a two-litre bottle of vodka.**

114 **It was the wife's birthday so I went into Ann Summers and said, "Have you got a see-through nighty please?" She said, "What size?" I said, "58-49-65." She said, "Are you sure you want to see through to that?"**

115 **My wife used to have a hourglass figure....but the sands of time have shifted a bit....I said to her, "You've put on a lot of weight." "No I haven't", she said. I thought, 'I'm gonna win this one'......I said, "You used to be 7lb 4 oz."**

116 **The wife said she wanted something that does 0-60 in 5 seconds for Christmas, hint, hint......... I've bought her a set of bathroom scales.**

117 **It takes an awful lot of balls to play golf badly.**

118 **My girlfriend bought a cook book 'Cheap and Easy Vegetarian Cooking'. It's ideal because not only is she a vegetarian but..........**

119 **I always wanted to be a comedian but was scared of being laughed at.**

120 **To spice things up in the bedroom I went on Amazon and bought '101 Mating Positions'. My sex life's still crap but my chess has improved.**

VIDEO 5

Jokes 85 to 120 can all be viewed at this Video Link.

The Videos referred to in this book are all recorded from Christmas Revue shows at Kenilworth Golf Club. After many years of Friday then Saturday performances, the entire revue team never ceased to be amazed how much audiences varied. The identical material and the same list of jokes, that might go down a storm on the Friday showing, could be a real struggle on the Saturday.

In this Video the cast have clearly asked me to 'ask the audience to liven up'. Obviously, this is not an ideal approach since you are effectively saying "please laugh because last night the audience laughed a lot!" →

→ In the show I am explaining to the audience "I need to test how bright you are, because if you're not bright you're not going to get these jokes because they're good, they're very good". Immediately a heckler pops up with "they had better be better than last year's Simmo" .... to which I have a ready response of "yes.... I remember my first drink Malcolm!"

Once the performance warms up all goes well with plenty of banter. The rounding off joke is:

A traffic warden's funeral. Crowded around the graveside the Vicar throws a handful of soil on the coffin in the normal way...just then there's this little voice coming from the coffin saying "I'm still alive, help, let me out". The vicar says "sorry luv, I've already started the paperwork!"

121 **The wife's been really helpful to me, otherwise I would have thought I had no faults.**

122 **I've just been given two weeks to live......why are you smiling?......well, what I mean is the wife's going away to her sister's for two weeks.**

123 **I'm a solo trapeze artist, I used to have a partner but I had to let him go.**

124 **I'd like to have a sex change....from none to absolutely loads.**

125 **I've changed my bank password to 'incorrect', now if I forget it reminds me 'your password is incorrect'......... how good is that?**

126 **A kid swallowed some coins. His mum phoned the hospital to see how he was doing. "No change yet," said the hospital.**

127 **On a first date I tend to ask about the street she grew up in, her first pets, birthday, that sort of thing....at least then if I don't get anywhere I'll have access to her passwords.**

128 **After 5 karate lessons I can now break a two-inch thick bread board with my plaster cast.**

129 **I saw a billboard poster saying "Learn to read". I thought, who are they aiming that poster at?**

130 **The trouble with jogging is that by the time you realise you're not in shape for it, it's too far to walk back.**

131 **Why have health food, at my age I need all the preservatives I can get.**

132 **I'm not vegetarian but I eat animals that are.**

133 **A cat hijacked a plane and said, "Take me to the Canaries."**

134 **A man has been jailed for assaulting a fortune teller who predicted he would go to jail.**

135 **You know you are getting old when everything either dries up or leaks.**

136 **I ate a chess set. It tasted horrible so I took it back to the shop. I said, "It's stale mate". He said, "Are you sure?" I said, "Check mate."**

137 **Apparently 9 out of 10 single women who sit at home and have conversations with their cats are mentally disturbed. My dog's full of useful information like that.**

138 **I saw Sky News showing the riots in Greece, the whole place looks like it's in ruins.**

139 **I've got a new app for my mobile phone. It's a phone box locator!**

140 **I saw a sign on the maternity room door. It said, 'Push, push, push.'**

141 **I bought a brand new boomerang, but I don't seem to be able to throw the old one away.**

142 **I do 5 sit-ups every morning, it might not sound much but there are only so many times you can hit the snooze button.**

143 **Why couldn't Joseph and Mary get in at the inn? ....It was Christmas!**

144 **Claiming disability benefit isn't as easy as you think. You have to jump through quite a few hoops.**

145 **To get your proper weight really you need to strip off completely......mind you, they weren't happy in Boots.**

146 **Our dog can find everything.......he's a 'labragoogle'.**

147 **My missus is a stunner.........well I say that; she's got a new job down at the abattoir.**

148 **A container ship full of blue paint has collided into a ship full of red paint. The crew have been marooned.**

149 **Remember boys and girls, do not handle any fireworks, leave it to the adults who have been drinking all day.**

150 **I lost my pet mouse 'Elvis' yesterday....he was 'caught in a trap' and couldn't get out.**

151 **The train was ever so busy; even all the men couldn't get seats.**

152 **Last year's show was a great success but the audience was a failure.**

153 **I was very big in the cement business; I was a great mixer.**

154 **The wife said, "Simmo you're rubbish in bed", so as a special surprise for her, two very nice girls have been helping me train to improve......**

155 **Why can't life's problems hit us when we are 18 and know everything?**

156 **I've just bought a pair of binoculars, really pricey, £900. I reckon the guy saw me coming.**

157 **I said, Doctor, I want some sleeping pills for my wife. He said, "Why?" I said, "She's woken up."**

158 **Knock knock. Who's there? It's me, Grandpa..... wait, stop the funeral!**

159 **The trouble with the girls in our house is that they always forget to leave the toilet seat up.**

160 **Doctor Doctor I'm scared of Father Christmas....don't worry, you're just a little claustrophobic.**

161 **I won't rest until I find a cure for insomnia.**

162 **Apparently the Houses of Parliament are infected with vermin......at least that's what the rats are saying.**

163 **My husband and I divorced over religious differences. He thought he was God and I didn't.**

164 **If you ever feel the world is moving too fast, take comfort from the queue at the supermarket checkout.**

165 **If ASDA lower prices every day why isn't anything in the shop free yet?**

166 **Yesterday the man died who invented predictive text. His funfair is next monkey.**

167 **The wife said she suspected me of being a transvestite......so I packed her things and left.**

168 **I tried to get rid of my old boomerang by throwing it really, really hard.......now I live in constant fear.**

169 **The wife's on a diet of coconuts and bananas......she hasn't lost any weight but she can't half climb trees.**

170 **My wife texted me after a row to say I was very condescending. To be honest I was surprised she even could spell it.**

171 **I went to the doctor. I said, "I keep seeing double". He said, "Take a seat in the chair." I said, "Which one?"**

172 **What do diarrhoea and electric cars have in common? ....Will I make it home?**

173 **We've had a letter from Bill Bailey.......he's decided to come home.**

174 **I don't drink, don't smoke, don't womanise all night; but things will change when I get out of prison.**

175 **I slept through the alarm this morning, luckily it was only a small fire.**

176 **I was gonna tell a joke about time-travelling. But you guys didn't like it.**

177 **You never open the leaflet on a packet of pills and it says something good like, 'May cause extreme sexiness'.**

178 **My advice in life is to give everything 100%.....unless you're giving blood.**

179 **What would you do if you saw an endangered animal eating an endangered plant?**

180 **Why is it so hard for women to find men that are sensitive, caring and attractive? Those men already have boyfriends.**

181 **Why can't your hand be 12 inches long? Because then it'd be a foot.**

182 **The mother-in-law came round unexpectedly yesterday..............that's the last time I buy cheap chloroform.**

183 **Some days I have to take three or four baths to make the phone ring.**

184 **Doctor, Doctor, I feel like a pack of cards. "I'll deal with you later."**

185 **What was the best thing before they invented sliced bread?**

186 **Recipes are like online dating sites.....they never end up looking like the pictures.**

187 **The wife says I'm nosey and intrusive.....at least that's what it says in her diary.**

188 **Have you ever noticed that anyone going slower than you is an idiot, and anyone going faster is a maniac?**

189 **Bloke at an auction bought a parrot. He says to the auctioneer, "I paid an awful lot of money for this parrot but I never even checked if it could talk." The auctioneer responded, " I wouldn't worry too much about that Sir.....who do you think was bidding against you?"**

190 **A woman on trial for beating him over the head with his guitar collection. The Judge asks, "First offender?" She says, "No, first a Gibson, then a Fender".**

191 **I went online and bought a DVD on 'How to handle disappointment'. When I opened it, it was empty.**

192 **The most common lie from a Welshman is, "I was only trying to help that sheep over the fence."**

193 **The boss of Ryanair walks into a bar thinking Guinness at £2 pint is cheap. The barman smiles and says, "Would you like a glass with that?"**

194 **A study has shown that women who carry a little weight tend to live longer than men who mention it.**

195 **My wife's from Scotland, she loves summer. It used to be her favourite day of the year.**

196 **Shoplifting from an Apple store strictly speaking should just count as scrumping.**

197 **I read that men who make love 4 times a week live on average 12 years longer than men who don't. I said to the wife, "You're trying to kill me." She said, "No, it sounds like you're trying to kill me."**

198 **I used to sell Filofaxes to the mafia; I was involved in very organised crime.**

199 **The main difference between Dubai and Abu Dhabi is that people in Dubai don't like The Flintstones, but people in Abu Dhabidoooo.**

200 **I read an article which says typical signs of stress are, eating too much, impulse buying and driving too fast ....my idea of a perfect day!**

201 **Some woman described me the other day as 'A bit of a looker'. Well I say that........creepy voyeur were her actual words.**

202 **Why is it called Alcoholics Anonymous when the first thing you do is stand up and say, "I'm an alcoholic and my name's Simon"?**

203 **I went to the ballet once; I couldn't even tell who won.**

204 **I was sitting in a restaurant and suddenly got hit on the head by a prawn cocktail. I turned around and this big guy shouts, "And that's just for starters."**

205 **Did you know, towels are the biggest cause of dry skin?**

206 **No matter how nice the soap smells, never leave a public toilet sniffing your fingers.**

207 **I sat in the pub with the missus, I looked at these two old buggers, I said, "That's us in ten years"...she said, "That's a mirror!"**

208 **Is it just me or does the moaning about Christmas beginning earlier every year begin earlier every year?**

209 **Warm baths do NOT cure insomnia; two bottles of red wine cure insomnia.**

210 **I told the doctor I was suffering from insomnia he said, "Don't lose any sleep over it."**

211 **The local cinema owner has died; the funeral with be at 2.00, 4.40, 6.00 and 7.30.**

212 **Knock knock. Who's there? Dyslexia. Dyslexia how?**

213 **Every new McDonald's creates 20 new jobs - 10 dentists, 10 heart surgeons.**

214 **Why do frisbees get larger the closer they get?.....then it hit me.**

215 **Healthy people are just dying more slowly.**

216 **My mate was run over by a steam roller. The nurse said he's in ward 15,16 and 17.**

217 **Never under any circumstances take a laxative and a sleeping pill at the same time.**

218 **I think I must be in a 'same sex relationship'........put it another way, after 20 years the sex is just the same.**

219 **My nephew just rang to say he just got 17 GCSE's all at A grade; only ones he failed were Maths and English.**

220 **I got a new job as a waiter, the pay's rubbish but at least it puts food on the table.**

221 **Incredible to think every Scotsman started out as a scotch egg!**

222 **My lesbian neighbours gave me a Rolex; I think they misunderstood me when I said, I wanna watch!**

223 **I've got a stalker...everywhere I go she's there 10 paces in front of me.**

224 **I just missed a hole-in-one by 6 shots.**

225 **Hey kids, try the new social media networking tool ... it's called 'outside'.**

226 **At Alton Towers it's always fun to bring a few nuts and bolts out of your pocket and show them to the person sitting next to you once the ride has begun.**

227 **I always keep a bottle of wine in the fridge for special occasions....like Thursdays.**

228 **I'm a sex object.......I suggest sex and she objects.**

229 **It's funny when a magician needs to sneeze, he can't get his hanky out quick enough because it's always 3 feet long.**

230 **Doctor: "The best thing you can do is give up drinking and smoking and start eating healthy food." Patient: "What's the second best thing?"**

231 **Telesales people ring you saying, "Do you want cheap gas?" I say, "No, when it comes to gas it's quality I'm looking for."**

232 **I went to the doctor, I said, "I've got a load of £20 notes stuck up my backside." He had a dig around..... (sorry too graphic......) then he said, "Blimey I've found 1980 pounds." I said, "I told you I wasn't feeling two grand."**

233 **Always read the instructions on the Viagra box and never take more that the recommended dose; trust me I found out the hard way.**

234 **A chicken walks up to a duck who is about to cross the road. He says, "Don't do it mate you'll never hear the end of it."**

235 **After years of trying to figure women out, I'm moving on to much simpler subjects - like quantum physics.**

236 **What do you call it when you lose an Italian sausage......... a falsalami.**

237 **A Frenchman's just created a 20ft tall dessert of fruit, jelly and sponge....he called it the trifle tower.**

238 **I said to my son will you please stop watching porn, your mother and me can hear it in the next room. He said, "Dad it's Maria Sharapova at Wimbledon."**

239 **The wife spent two hours at the beautician's yesterday, they didn't actually do anything, they were just preparing the estimate.**

240 **I love a bargain....... we've got a back garden full of shopping trolleys.....they're only a pound each.**

241 **Spent half my time at school scared of fractions ...... well I say half.**

242 **Anne Robinson's left the Weakest Link but her surgeon has put a brave face on her........**

243 **I never drink unless I am alone or with someone.**

244 **If a man says he'll fix something there's no need to remind him every six months.**

245 **Oysters are supposed to be good aphrodisiacs? I tried a dozen but only 3 of them worked.**

246 **I wonder what "Don't touch" is in Braille.**

247 **Andy Murray went into the library and asks for a couple of books on great tennis serves. The librarian says, "No, you'll never return them."**

248 **Golf pro to two ladies. "Are you here to learn to play golf?"......... "My friend is, I learnt yesterday!"**

249 **Did you hear about the ship carrying a consignment of yo-yos? .....It sank thirty-four times.**

250 **The Scots invented golf, I figure, these are the same people who think music comes out of bagpipes.**

251 **I think my days of acting in pantomime are behind me...........**

252 **My grandad was famous for inventing the first door knocker......he was awarded the Nobel Prize.**

253 **Don't be frightened of trying a bit of bondage........ maybe get someone to show you the ropes.**

254 **I don't know if I have ever tried a calorie but apparently they are delicious.**

255 **Doctor, Doctor! I've swallowed the film in my camera. We'll just have to wait and see what develops.**

256 **How can you spot the people who can't count to 10? They are the ones in front of you in the fast check-out lane.**

257 **The wife's threatening to leave me because apparently I'm a smart arse. She says the relationship is at a crossroads. One way is love and trust, the other is divorce. I said, "I think you'll find that is a T junction not a crossroads!"**

258 **Every time I hear of someone being attacked by a shark I think "Didn't they hear the music?"**

259 **How does Good King Wenceslas like his pizzas? Deep pan, crisp and even!!**

260 **I don't know what's best about Switzerland, but of course the flag's a big plus.**

261 **Tennis....all that grunting, we turn it up so the neighbours think we're having sex.**

262 **Doctor, Doctor! I keep thinking I'm a piece of chalk. "Well please get to the end of the cue."**

263 **I bought a leopard skin coat off Amazon......it was spotless when it arrived so I sent it back.**

264 **I bought some sleeping tablets. The label said, 'Warning. May cause drowsiness'.**

265 **I said to the wife, "There's a burglar downstairs in the kitchen eating that pie you made this afternoon." She said, "Ring 999." I said, "Shall I ask for the Police or an Ambulance?"**

266 **You can't always find exactly what you want on the Internet. I searched for cigarette lighters and got 10,000 matches.**

267 **These paperless offices are OK but what do you do when you go to the toilet?**

268 **I came here on a train tonight......passenger announcement: "This is a passenger announcement, the train that has just arrived at platform 1,2,3,4 &5 has come in sideways."**

269 **The wife went to the doctor with 'ladies things', she says he told her she needs to have sex 5 times a week........ I said, "Put me down for Mondays and Fridays."**

270 **If you don't want to go on holiday you can get the same effect by staying at home and tipping every second person you see.**

271 **Advent calendars; their days are numbered.**

272 **I said to the wife, "It isn't your jeans that make your bum look fat."**

273 **I've been stood up more times than a bowling pin.**

274 **The boss said to me, "In a rare moment I'm going to mix business with pleasure - you're fired."**

275 **A woman golfer was in court for beating her husband to death with a golf club. The judge asks, "How many times did you hit him with the club madam?" She said, "I can't remember whether it was 6 or 7 times; put me down for a 5."**

276 **A racehorse walks into a golf club with two men; the barman says to the horse, "You can't come in here, not with those trainers."**

277 **My doctor gave me a prescription for extra strength placebos.**

278 **Ironic....someone on Facebook saying 'get a life'.**

279 **I've got a new stopwatch ....0-60 in one minute.**

280 **The wife says I never listen to what she says....or something like that.**

281 **A Royal Engineer serving overseas wrote 200 letters a month to his girlfriend back home. This Saturday at All Saints Church she marries the postman.**

282 **I wondered "Do prostitutes have babies?" ....of course they do, where do you think traffic wardens come from?**

283 **Doctor, sometimes I think I'm a wigwam, sometimes I think I'm a teepee.......... the doctor says, "I think your trouble is that you're two tents."**

284 **The doctor told me to go outside more...so I took up smoking.**

285 **I wanted to be a barber....but I just couldn't cut it.**

286 **To impress new birds on a date I usually say to them I had a flat on Park Lane ....I miss out the bit about it being on my mountain bike.**

287 **Doctor Doctor my wife has lost her voice, what can I do to help her? He said, "Try coming home pissed at 3 o'clock in the morning."**

288 **My wife and I have an agreement. She does what she wants and I do what she wants.**

289 **Patient says, "Doctor the problem is that obesity runs in our family." He says, "No, the problem is nobody runs in your family."**

290 **She said she was approaching 40, but I couldn't help wondering from which direction?**

291 **Just as the coffin was being lowered into ground at the traffic warden's funeral, a voice inside yelled, "Help, help. I'm not dead, I'm not dead." The vicar shouted back, "I'm sorry but I've already started writing the paperwork."**

292 **Why do we all feel safe under the blankets? It's not like a murderer will come in thinking, "I'm gonna kill.... oh damn he's under a blanket."**

293 **I've put an electric fence around my back garden..... the neighbour's dead against it.**

294 **I said to this beautiful girl, "Hey gorgeous where have you been all my life?" She said, "For the first half of it I wasn't even alive!"**

295 **I don't mind people telling me they're gay, I just don't want them ramming it down my throat.**

296 **I used to be a builder for 175 years............... but that's just an estimate.**

297 **I once had a job interview to be a mustard cutter ....but I wasn't quite up to it.**

298 **Talk about luck. A bloke wins £120 million on the lottery and two days later meets the love of his life.**

299 **All this talk of genetically modified food being contrary to nature is utter rubbish...I've just had a delicious 'leg of cod'.**

300 **I love sat nav ...don't know where I'd be without it.**

301 **Doctor, Doctor! I think I'm a smoke detector. Well calm down there's no cause for alarm.**

302 **Waiter, what's this fly doing in my soup? It's fly soup Sir.**

303 **Two women standing at a funeral. "I blame myself for his death", said the wife. "Why?" said her friend. "Because I shot him!" said the wife.**

304 **People always complain about the weather but nobody does anything about it.**

305 **A boxer goes to a doctor complaining about insomnia. He's says, "Have you tried counting sheep?" The boxer says, "No good, every time I get to nine I stand up."**

306 **My doctor reckons I'm paranoid. He didn't say so, but I know what he's thinking.**

307 **My mate on the dodgems has lost his job. He's suing for 'funfair dismissal'!**

308 **The Doctor has prescribed me anti-hypochondria tablets, but I'm worried about the side effects.**

309 **How much does a grand piano cost? About £1000. (*a Grand!*)**

310 **You get these mountain climbers roping themselves together. It's in case one comes to his senses and wants to go home.**

311 **Doctor, Doctor I've got five you know what's......"How do your trousers fit?" asked the doctor. "No problem at all," said the guy. "They fit like a glove."**

312 **My boyfriend says the doctor wanted a urine sample, and faeces sample. I told him, "Just hand over your boxer shorts."**

313 **A man goes into a fish and chip shop and orders fish and chips twice. The owner says, "I heard you the first time."**

314 **My wife said, "Will you still love me when I'm old and ugly?" I said, "Of course I do."**

315 **Dead car batteries......don't get me started.**

316 **Just bought Pavarotti's old car....it's a Nissan Dorma.**

317 **Yesterday I had to put air in my tyres. It was a pound to use the machine. I remember when it was 10p. That's inflation for you.**

318 **Does anyone in the room know a Delilah? Or is it just Tom Jones?**

319 **I said to the wife, "Fancy a quicky?" She responded, "As opposed to what?"**

320 **I got a guitar delivered yesterday but it was addressed to someone else. I just wrote on the box, 'Return to Fender'.**

321 **An odd thing happened to me yesterday. I found a hat with some money in it. Next thing you know a bloke with a guitar is chasing me down the road.**

322 **Yesterday an ice cream van crashed into the back of my car when I was at the traffic lights. The doctor at the hospital said I had 'Whippy lash'.**

323 **My wife left me because of my terrible gambling habit....... But I'm looking at ways of winning her back.**

324 **Well girls, when you're lying on the beach wearing a bikini, the worst thing you can hear is "good for you".**

325 **My wife's leaving me because of my obsession with rugby. I keep pleading with her to give it one more try.**

326 **I just got back from my best friend's funeral. He died after he was struck on the head with a tennis ball. It was a lovely service.**

327 **Most people are shocked when they find out how bad I am as an electrician.**

328 **Last night my girlfriend was complaining that I never listen to her... or something like that.**

329 **A friend of mine owned a balloon company, but sadly he had to close it. Couldn't keep up with the cost of inflation.**

330 **I was addicted to the hokey cokey, but then I turned myself around.**

331 **My wife told me to stop impersonating a flamingo. I had to put my foot down.**

332 **Did you hear about the statistician who drowned while crossing a river? It was three feet deep on average.**

333 **I used to have a dog who liked red wine. He was a Bordeaux collie.**

334 **My next door neighbour has a green triangular house. My other next door neighbour has a yellow rectangular house. And the people across the road have an orange octagonal house... I live in a quality street.**

335 **Who was the first man to sail around the world single handed? Robin Knox Johnson? Sir Francis Chichester? ..... no.... Captain Hook!**

336 **If I come across any innuendo, I'll whip it out immediately.**

337 **Beastly weather occurs when it rains cats and dogs.**

338 **A cannibal is a man who sometimes has his friends for dinner.**

339 **Driverless cars......they're just around the corner.**

340 **He's been in the entertainment business for 30 years......and he's got the jokes to prove it.**

341 **He calls himself a rapid fire comedian....he should be fired rapidly.**

342 **She maybe an heiress, but she looks more like an heirloom.**

343 **The wife has always been so angry with me that she turned round the first time I whistled.**

344 **A man walks into a psychiatrist's wearing only cling film for shorts. The psychiatrist says, "Well I can clearly see you're nuts."**

345 **The world champion tongue twister got arrested. I hear they're going to give him a tough sentence.**

346 **The missus is always wanting to keep up with the Joneses: we've got a big square patio so she's had me paint it blue so all the people looking on Google Earth think we've got a swimming pool.**

347 **The guy said, "Would you like your pizza cut into 4 pieces or 8 pieces?" I said, "Crikey.....I couldn't eat 8 pieces."**

348 **A polar bear walks into a pub and asks for ....(long pause)......a pint of lager please. The barman says, "Why the big paws?"**

349 **I said to the missus, "Were you faking it last night?" She said, "No, I really was asleep."**

350 **Two men discussing sex. One says to the other, "Are you a 'oncer' or a 'twicer' "? "A 'twicer'," says the other guy. "Which do you prefer?" says the first man........ "Oh I think the winter one!" says the other bloke.**

351 **The wife said, "What would you call me if I said I was having sex with your best friend?" The husband replied, "A lesbian".**

352 **I got myself fitted with a pacemaker. Now every time I have sex with the missus, the garage door opens.**

353 **I said to the wife, "Shall we go on a world cruise?" She replied, "Can't we go somewhere else?"**

354 **I have a few jokes about unemployed people, but none of them work.**

355 **The wife's putting her foot down and says that's it, choose me or football. I said, "Give me 90 minutes to think about it!"**

356 **Maybe if we tell the teenagers their brain is an app they will start using it.**

357 **The man who invented Velcro has died........R.I.P.**

358 **I've been thinking about my career. Upon reflection, I could see myself working in a mirror factory. (Two jokes in one!)**

359 **I made the house completely childproof.........but they're still getting in.**

360 **I said to the pharmacist, "If I ask you for Viagra will I be able to get it over the counter?" She said, "You will if you take two!"**

361 **I said, Doctor I keep singing 'The Green, Green, Grass of Home'. He said, "You've got Tom Jones Syndrome". I said, "Is it common?" He replied "It's not unusual."**

362 **My son's always on his Playstation. I said, "Why don't you go outside for a while?" "It's raining," he grunted. I said, "Well it's your lucky day, they've just discovered that skin is waterproof!"**

363 **There has never been a fisherman who could keep both hands in his pockets when describing the one that got away.**

364 **What do you call a dog magician? A labracadabrador.**

365 **"What are your golf clubs doing here?" the bride asked at the altar. " This isn't going to take all day is it?" he said.**

Hecklers

For all comedians hecklers are going to be encountered at some point. Of course it's always sods law that hecklers tend to pop up when things are going badly already!

Most comedians give very little thought to how they are going to deal with a heckler thus I think it is worth giving the matter some attention.

The first rule is to stay calm and maintain your composure. The hecklers aim is to disrupt your performance. You have three options, these are to 'ignore, join or attack'.

If you 'ignore' it's unlikely to be the end of the matter but it might if the heckler is not too confident.

As a first response you may just choose to acknowledge the heckler and thank them for their input.

If you can 'comeback' with a decent 'putdown' then this will either go well and add to the fun, or further distract from your delivery. This can all add to the fun of the show. Keep it fun. You cannot afford for it to turn into a fight at all costs so it needs to have a friendly resolution at all costs.

The really good news is that hecklers usually irritate audiences, thus if your 'comeback' is sharp and witty you will easily get the audience appreciative and onside.

Preparation is key in how you are going to handle the situation. We have listed plenty of top quality 'put downs' that should really put you in a good situation when the inevitable happens; ENJOY!

Retorts to a Heckler

1. I remember when I had my first pint.
2. You bring everyone so much joy when you leave a room.
3. I'd give you a nasty look but you've already got one.
4. You must be good at skiing, you've been going downhill for 30 years.
5. Remember when I asked for your opinion? Me neither.
6. Someday you'll go far. I hope you stay there.
7. You're impossible to underestimate.
8. I don't know what your problem is, but I'm guessing it's hard to pronounce.
9. I don't have the time or the crayons to explain this to you.
10. I love what you've done with your hair. How do you get it to come out of the nostrils like that?
11. The problem isn't that obesity runs in your family. It's that no-one runs in your family.

12 **If ignorance is bliss, you must be the happiest person on the planet.**

13 **Hold still. I'm trying to imagine you with a personality.**

14 **You'll never be the man your mum is.**

15 **I'm not insulting you, I'm describing you.**

16 **Don't be ashamed of who you are.**
That's your parents' job.

17 **A million sperm.....and you were the fastest.**

18 **Thanks Sir.......I normally work alone....**

19 **Are you circumcised? If you are they threw the wrong bit in the bucket!**

20 **I know you were disappointed to get to London**
and find Big Ben was a clock.......!
(an aside to a woman)

A Joke to ruin the day!

Before I start ladies and gentlemen, let us observe a few moments silence in memory of the 3,000 prawns, 200 chickens, countless carnations, delphiniums, lilies and roses who selflessly gave their lives to make this wedding celebration possible.

Amusing Quotations

There is no shortage in the world of excellent quotations. Throughout my life I have always kept a computer file with some of my favourites and here they are for your enjoyment. Obviously when preparing a comedy act there is no reason not to use them in your material but being sure to credit the author.

Father told me that if ever I met a lady in a dress like yours, I must look her straight in the eyes.

(KING CHARLES IN PRINCE CHARLES DAYS)

It's a funny kind of month, October. For the real cricket fan it's when you discover that your wife left you in May. (DENIS NORDEN)

I'm not against naked girls - not as often as I'd like to be.

(BENNY HILL)

My wife wants Olympic sex - once every four years.

(RODNEY DANGERFIELD)

Vote for you? I'd sooner put my genitals in a pan of boiling chip fat. (VICTOR MELDREW, ONE FOOT IN THE GRAVE)

Neil Harvey's at slip, with his legs apart, waiting for a tickle.

(BRIAN JOHNSTON)

The best etiquette for getting off a crowded train against a crowd of people forcing their way on is to shout, "Excuse me, I think I'm going to be sick." (FRAN COLLINS)

A nation to try to tax itself into prosperity is like a man standing in a bucket and trying to lift himself by the handle.

(WINSTON CHURCHILL)

What are you most looking for after your cricket tour of India?..... A dry fart. **(PHIL EDMUNDS)**

He was a womaniser - as opposed to a woman who behaves like this who is not a maniser, but a right old slapper. **(JO BRAND)**

I'll ruin you. You'll never waitress in Torquay again.

(BASIL FAWLTY TO POLLY - FAWLTY TOWERS)

Too bad that all those people who really know how to run the country are busy driving taxi cabs and cutting hair.

(GEORGE BURNS)

Middle-age is when you look at the rain teeming down and say, "That'll be good for the garden." **(GRACE MARSHALL)**

The best way to remember your wife's birthday is to forget it once. **(E JOSEPH CROSSMAN)**

When I look back at my life, my happiest memory is not 'the goons' but a girl named Julia with big hooters. **(SPIKE MILLIGAN)**

If you resolve to give up smoking, drinking and sex, you don't live longer - it just seems longer. **(CLEMENT FREUD)**

The Commandments don't tell you what you ought to do - they just put ideas in your head. **(ELIZABETH BIBESCO)**

After the game, the king and the pawn go in the same box.

(ITALIAN PROVERB)

Lost: black and white dog, blind in left eye, half of right ear missing, no tail, limps. Answers to the name of Lucky.
(NEWSPAPER ADVERT)

A woman's rule of thumb: if it has tyres or testicles you're going to have trouble with it. (ELLA GOUGH)

The only reason they say 'Women and children first", is to test the strength of the lifeboats. (JEAN KERR)

The trouble with women is that they never put the toilet seat back up. (SIMON NYE)

They say a women's work is never done. All I'm saying is if you organised yourself a bit better..... (JIMMY CARR)

If you think women are the weaker sex, try pulling the duvet back to your side. (Stuart Turner)

Men are superior to women. For example they can urinate from a speeding car. (WILL DURST)

Sexualities are very confusing. As I understand it transvestites are the ones that grow down from the ceiling, and transsexuals are the ones that grow up. (PAMELA YAGER)

"So Debbie Magee, what first attracted you to the millionaire Paul Daniels?" (MRS MERTON)

I remember the first time I had sex, because I kept the receipt.
(BILL BRANDIS)

You know that look women get when they want sex......no me neither. (DREW CAREY)

'Listen carefully', or 'Sexual perversion' (5,2,4,4)
(CROSSWORD CLUE FINANCIAL TIMES) Answer: Prick up your ears.

When a man talks dirty to a woman it's sexual harassment. When a woman talks dirty to a man it's £10 per minute. (STEVEN WRIGHT)

Oh yes, I've tried my hand at sex. (EMO PHILIPS)

I've been chased before by women, but never when I was awake. (BOB HOPE)

If he hasn't called you in 3 weeks and you have no idea where he is, chances are he's not moaning your name in the emergency room. (DIANE CONWAY)

I got married again last year, because my first wife died in a wishing well. (TONY GERRARD)

The main purpose of children's parties is to remind you that there are children worse than your own. (KATHARINE WHITEHORN)

Santa Claus has the right idea. Visit people once a year. (VICTOR BORGE)

I play Cinderella tennis, that is, I don't quite get to the ball. (LARRY ADLER)

I've got a good feel for the game of golf. I did very well on the course at Skegness, until I got stuck in one of those little wooden windmills. (RIGSBY - RISING DAMP)

My hamster died yesterday. Fell asleep at the wheel. (FRANK CARSON)

I don't accept your dog's admiration as conclusive proof that you are wonderful. (ANN LANDERS)

I'm an environmentalist. Most of my jokes are recycled.
(DAVID LETTERMAN)

When is 'Last Night of the Proms' going to mean it? (DANNY BHOY)

Muzak in pubs and hotel foyers seeps around like nerve gas.
(WILLIAM MCILVANNEY)

What's the difference between a bagpipe and an onion? Nobody cries when you chop up a bagpipe. (ANON)

The Rolling Stones have announced a new tour. Fans will recognise their tour bus as the one doing forty in the fast lane with the indicator on. (KEVIN NEALON)

The hardest thing about writing country music must be thinking up clean words that rhyme with 'truck'. (BRIAN KAUFMAN)

I've seen him entertain fifty times and I've always enjoyed his joke. (JONNY CARSON)

The first thing a comedian does on getting an unscheduled laugh, is to check his buttons. (ALVA JOHNSON)

Before we got engaged he never farted; now it's a second language. (CAROLINE RHEA)

The worst words in the English language are, "We need to talk". Either that or, "Who's bra is this?" (JERRY SEINFELD)

Fragile is usually interpreted by postal workers as 'throw underarm'. (HARRY HERSHFIELD)

I think the expression 'it's a small world' is really a euphemism for 'I keep running into people I can't stand'. (BROCK COHEN)

What's another word for thesaurus? **(STEPHEN WRIGHT)**

The batsman's holding the bowler's willy. **(BRIAN JOHNSTONE)**

The human brain starts working the minute you're born and never stops until you stand up to speak in public. **(GEORGE JESSEL)**

The quickest way to make a red light turn green is to try to find something in the glove compartment. **(BILLY CONNOLLY)**

My wife came home and said I have some good news and some bad news. I said, "Give me the good news." She said, "The airbag works." **(ROY CHUBBY BROWN)**

When buying a car, try all the buttons on the radio. If they are all rock 'n roll there's a good chance the transmission is shot. **(LARRY LUJAC)**

Sir, Saturday morning, although recurring at regular and predictable intervals, always seems to take this station by surprise. **(W S GILBERT)**

Mr Speaker, I withdraw my statement that half the cabinet are asses. Half the cabinet are not asses. **(BENJAMIN DISRAELI)**

I think the voters mis-underestimate me. **(GEORGE W BUSH)**

Governments are like underpants. They need to be changed often and for the same reason. **(ITALIAN PROVERB)**

The best argument against democracy is a five-minute conversation with the average voter. **(WINSTON CHURCHILL)**

Has anyone been caught thieving in the Middle East? Let's have a show of hands. **(JIMMY CARR)**

We live in an age where pizza gets to your house far quicker than the Police. (JEFF MARDER)

I lent a friend of mine £10,000 for plastic surgery and now I don't know what he looks like. (EMO PHILIPS)

George Best, do you think if you hadn't had to do all that running around on a football field, you wouldn't have got so thirsty? (MRS MERTON)

You can live to a hundred if you give up all the things that make you want to live to a hundred. (WOODY ALLEN)

Our gardener passed away. He had a heart attack cutting the elaborate maze hedge. The paramedics never stood a chance. (NILES CRANE)

My cousin died. He was stung by a wasp......the natural enemy of a tightrope walker. (EMO PHILIPS)

The only reason so many turned up at his funeral was to make sure he was dead. (SAMUEL GOLDWYN)

When you buy a V-necked sweater there's a V of material missing. Do you know what they do with that? They send it to Ann Summers and she makes those fancy pants. (HARRY HILL)

Do I examine myself for testicular cancer? I do, but I do it on the train. (ARTHUR SMITH)

A good sermon should be like a woman's skirt; short enough to arouse interest but long enough to cover the essentials. (RONALD KNOX)

Category 365

In this section we have listed the one-liners in Category Order. We hope that you might find this useful if sourcing material for a specific subject area. ENJOY!

Animal	1	**A polar bear walks into a pub and asks for ....(long pause)......a pint of lager please. The barman says, "Why the big paws?"**
Builders	2	**I used to be a builder for 175 years............... but that's just an estimate.**
Canary	3	**A cat hijacked a plane and said, "Take me to the Canaries."**
	4	**A sign outside a pet shop 'Dead canary for sale - not going cheap'.**
Cannibal	5	**A cannibal is a man who sometimes has his friends for dinner.**
	6	**Two cannibals eating a clown. One says to the other "Does he taste funny to you?"**
	7	**Two cannibals eating meal. One says to the other, "Your wife makes a lovely meal." The other says, "Yes, I'm going to miss her."**

8 **Did you hear about the cannibal in a restaurant.....he ordered the waiter!**

9 **Father-and-son cannibals are in the jungle. Suddenly they spot a beautiful girl. The son says, "Dad let's eat her." The father replies, "No, let's take her home and eat your mother!"**

Christmas

10 **I'm doing my bit to help the homeless this Christmas, I've got stacks of cardboard boxes to give away.**

11 **Why couldn't Joseph and Mary get in at the inn? ....It was Christmas!**

12 **Is it just me or does the moaning about Christmas beginning earlier every year begin earlier every year?**

13 **How does Good King Wenceslas like his pizzas? Deep pan, crisp and even!!**

14 **Advent calendars; their days are numbered.**

Circus

15 **I was in the circus for many years; well I say 'in the circus'; I was the only one who could get the tent back in the bag.** **(MICK MILLER)**

16 **I was a human cannon ball for a while but the pay's crap......... sixty quid a week plus a bit of mileage.** **(MICK MILLER)**

17 **The contortionist at the circus has died suddenly................he died in his own arms.**

(MICK MILLER)

18 **My background is very much in the circus......... I came from a long line of conga dancers.**

19 **My brother had a great act on stilts....... I always looked up to him.**

20 **I'm a solo trapeze artist, I used to have a partner but I had to let him go.**

Comedian

21 **I always wanted to be a comedian but was scared of being laughed at.**

22 **He calls himself a rapid fire comedian.... he should be fired rapidly.**

Dad

23 **My dad was a roofer. He's not with us anymore. So Dad.....if you're up there......** **(MICK MILLER)**

24 **My dad had a weird hobby; collecting empty bottles; which sounds much better than saying he was an alcoholic.** **(MICK MILLER)**

25 **My dad knew when he was going to die......... the judge told him.** **(MICK MILLER)**

26 **My dad was sentenced to the electric chair. Anniversaries are difficult....we just put a wreath by the plug socket.** **(MICK MILLER)**

27 **My Dad died eating a bowl of Cheerios..... choked on one......we never got the chance to say goodbye.** **(MICK MILLER)**

Dating

28 **Recipes are like online dating sites.....they never end up looking like the pictures.**

29 **I've been stood up more times than a bowling pin.**

30 **To impress new birds on a date I usually say to them I had a flat on Park Lane ....I miss out the bit about it being on my mountain bike.**

Doctor

31 **Doctor Doctor, I get heartburn every time I eat birthday cake. "Well take the candles off next time."**

32 **I saw the doctor, he said, "You've only got 10 to live." I said, "10 what.....years, months, days??".... He said, " 9. 8. 7. ...."**

33 **Doctor, I keep thinking that I'm a bell. "Well take these and if it doesn't clear up give me a ring."**

34 **Doctor, I keep seeing fish. Have you seen an optician? "No," I said, "I keep seeing fish, not opticians!"**

35 **Doctor I keep sleep walking. Well go home, take these and sprinkle them on the floor. Are they tablets to make me sleep? No, they're tin tacks!**

36 **Doctor I think I'm a moth. Why are you seeing me not a psychiatrist? Well your light was on.**

37 **A man walked in to the doctor's with a lettuce leaf sticking out of his ear. The doctor says, "That's strange." The man said, "That's just the tip of the iceberg."**

38 **I went to the doctor for a check-up. He said, "Have you had sex in the last 7 days?" I said, "Doctor, my birthday's in July...."**

39 **Doctor I think I'm suffering from low self-esteem. He said, "Don't worry too much, it's very common amongst total losers".**

40 **I said, Doctor I keep having this urge to paint myself gold. He said it was a guilt complex.**

41 **Doctor Doctor I keep seeing images of Donald Duck and Mickey Mouse. How long have you been having these Disney spells?**

42 **An old lady goes to the doctor's and says, "Doctor I keep doing these silent farts." The doctor says, "Well when is this happening?" The old lady says, "All the time Doctor, I've just done a silent fart right now". The doctor says, "Right, first we're going to get you a new hearing aid."**

43 **I said, Doctor, I want some sleeping pills for my wife. He said, "Why?" I said, "She's woken up."**

44 **Doctor Doctor I'm scared of Father Christmas.... don't worry, you're just a little claustrophobic.**

45 **I went to the doctor. I said, "I keep seeing double". He said, "Take a seat in the chair." I said, "Which one?"**

46 **Doctor, Doctor, I feel like a pack of cards. "I'll deal with you later."**

47 **I told the doctor I was suffering from insomnia he said, "Don't lose any sleep over it."**

48 **Doctor: "The best thing you can do is give up drinking and smoking and start eating healthy food." Patient: "What's the second best thing?"**

49 **I went to the doctor, I said, "I've got a load of £20 notes stuck up my backside." He had a dig around.....(sorry too graphic......) then he said, "Blimey I've found 1980 pounds." I said, "I told you I wasn't feeling two grand."**

50 **Doctor, Doctor! I've swallowed the film in my camera. We'll just have to wait and see what develops.**

51 **Doctor, Doctor! I keep thinking I'm a piece of chalk. "Well please get to the end of the cue."**

52 **My doctor gave me a prescription for extra strength placebos.**

53 **Doctor, sometimes I think I'm a wigwam, sometimes I think I'm a teepee.......... the doctor says, "I think your trouble is that you're two tents."**

54 **The doctor told me to go outside more...so I took up smoking.**

55 **Doctor Doctor my wife has lost her voice, what can I do to help her? He said, "Try coming home pissed at 3 o'clock in the morning."**

56 **Patient says, "Doctor the problem is that obesity runs in our family." He says, "No, the problem is nobody runs in your family."**

57 **Doctor, Doctor! I think I'm a smoke detector. Well calm down there's no cause for alarm.**

58 **A boxer goes to a doctor complaining about insomnia. He's says, "Have you tried counting sheep?" The boxer says, "No good, every time I get to nine I stand up."**

59 **My doctor reckons I'm paranoid. He didn't say so, but I know what he's thinking.**

60 **The Doctor has prescribed me anti-hypochondria tablets, but I'm worried about the side effects.**

61 **Doctor, Doctor I've got five you know what's... ..."How do your trousers fit?" asked the doctor. "No problem at all," said the guy. "They fit like a glove."**

Dog

62 **We've got a new dog called Rolex. He's a watch dog.**

63 **Our dog can find everything.......he's a 'labragoogle'.**

64 **I used to have a dog who liked red wine. He was a Bordeaux collie.**

65 **What do you call a dog magician? A labracadabrador.**

66 **Apparently 9 out of 10 single women who sit at home and have conversations with their cats are mentally disturbed. My dog's full of useful information like that.**

Drink

67 **I always keep a bottle of wine in the fridge for special occasions....like Thursdays.**

68 **I never drink unless I am alone or with someone.**

Education

69 **My nephew just rang to say just he got 17 GCSE's all at A grade; only ones he failed were Maths and English.**

70 **Spent half my time at school scared of fractions ......well I say half.**

71 **Teacher says to Jonny "Give me two pronouns." Jonny says, " What, me"?**

Energy

72 **When the phone goes "Do you want to change your energy supplier?", I find the best reply is, "No, I'm quite happy with food."**

73 **Telesales people ring you saying, "Do you want cheap gas?" I say, "No, when it comes to gas it's quality I'm looking for."**

Enter-tainment	74	**Last year's show was a great success but the audience was a failure.**
	75	**I think my days of acting in pantomime are behind me...........**
	76	**He's been in the entertainment business for 30 years......and he's got the jokes to prove it.**
	77	**I was addicted to the hokey cokey, but then I turned myself around.**
Feminist	78	**We get a lot of these militant feminists these days, I take my hat off to them....they don't like that.**
Film	79	**I hear there's a new Hollywood blockbuster called 'Constipated'............it hasn't come out yet.**
Fitness	80	**I do 5 sit-ups every morning, it might not sound much but there are only so many times you can hit the snooze button.**
Food	81	**In Egypt, archaeologists have found a mummy covered in nuts and chocolate chips........they think they have found the original Pharaoh Rocher.**
	82	**My girlfriend bought a cook book 'Cheap and Easy Vegetarian Cooking'. It's ideal because not only is she a vegetarian but..........**

83 **Why have health food, at my age I need all the preservatives I can get.**

84 **I'm not vegetarian but I eat animals that are.**

85 **I ate a chess set. It tasted horrible so I took it back to the shop. I said, "It's stale mate". He said, "Are you sure?" I said, "Check mate."**

86 **I was sitting in a restaurant and suddenly got hit on the head by a prawn cocktail. I turned around and this big guy shouts, "And that's just for starters."**

87 **What do you call it when you lose an Italian sausage......... a falsalami.**

88 **A Frenchman's just created a 20ft tall dessert of fruit, jelly and sponge....he called it the trifle tower.**

89 **I don't know if I have ever tried a calorie but apparently they are delicious.**

90 **All this talk of genetically modified food being contrary to nature is utter rubbish...I've just had a delicious 'leg of cod'.**

91 **Waiter, what's this fly doing in my soup? It's fly soup Sir.**

92 **A man goes into a fish and chip shop and orders fish and chips twice. The owner says, "I heard you the first time."**

93 **Yesterday an ice cream van crashed into the back of my car when I was at the traffic lights. The doctor at the hospital said I had 'Whippy lash'.**

94 **The guy said, "Would you like your pizza cut into 4 pieces or 8 pieces?" I said, "Crikey.....I couldn't eat 8 pieces."**

Funeral

95 **The local cinema owner has died; the funeral with be at 2.00, 4.40, 6.00 and 7.30.**

96 **Just as the coffin was being lowered into ground at the traffic warden's funeral, a voice inside yelled, "Help, help. I'm not dead, I'm not dead." The vicar shouted back, "I'm sorry but I've already started writing the paperwork."**

97 **Two women standing at a funeral. "I blame myself for his death", said the wife. "Why?" said her friend. "Because I shot him!" said the wife.**

98 **I just got back from my best friend's funeral. He died after he was struck on the head with a tennis ball. It was a lovely service.**

Golf

99 **It takes an awful lot of balls to play golf badly.**

100 **I just missed a hole-in-one by 6 shots.**

101 **Golf pro to two ladies. "Are you here to learn to play golf?"......... "My friend is, I learnt yesterday!"**

102 **The Scots invented golf, I figure, these are the same people who think music comes out of bagpipes.**

103 **A woman golfer was in court for beating her husband to death with a golf club. The judge asks, "How many times did you hit him with the club madam?" She said, "I can't remember whether it was 6 or 7 times; put me down for a 5."**

104 **"What are your golf clubs doing here?" the bride asked at the altar. " This isn't going to take all day is it?" he said.**

Health

105 **Someone threw a bottle of omega 3 at me and hit me in the face. The doctor said, "Luckily you've only got super-fish-oil injuries."**

106 **Viagra is now available in powdered form to put in your coffee. It doesn't help your sex life but it stops your biscuits going soft.**

107 **My mate Gav had terrible indigestion and he's died of an overdose of heartburn tablets. I can't believe that Gav-is-gone.**

108 **A lorry carrying a big delivery of Vicks nasal spray has turned over on the M6..... police are warning motorists to expect no congestion for at least 8 hours.**

109 **I went to see a psychic yesterday, he said, "What's your name?"..... I said, "I want my money back."**

110 **I want congratulate the Viagra Pharmaceutical Company, they had record sales of 2 million tablets last month......well done lads, keep it up.**

111 **You've heard of 'Wash and Go' shampoo. There's a new one out now for down and outs, it's called 'Go and Wash'.**

112 **A kid swallowed some coins. His mum phoned the hospital to see how he was doing. "No change yet," said the hospital.**

113 **You know you are getting old when everything either dries up or leaks.**

114 **Claiming disability benefit isn't as easy as you think. You have to jump through quite a few hoops.**

115 **To get your proper weight really you need to strip off completely......mind you, they weren't happy in Boots.**

116 **You never open the leaflet on a packet of pills and it says something good like, 'May cause extreme sexiness'.**

117 **My advice in life is to give everything 100%..... unless you're giving blood.**

118 **Did you know, towels are the biggest cause of dry skin?**

119 **Warm baths do NOT cure insomnia; two bottles of red wine cure insomnia.**

120 **Every new McDonald's creates 20 new jobs - 10 dentists, 10 heart surgeons.**

121 **Healthy people are just dying more slowly.**

122 **Never under any circumstances take a laxative and a sleeping pill at the same time.**

Horse racing

123 **A racehorse walks into a golf club with two men; the barman says to the horse, "You can't come in here, not with those trainers."**

Internet

124 **That eBay's good, I sold my homing pigeon 8 times last month.**

125 **Apple is merging with Blackberry; they're bringing out a new electronic device....it's called The Crumble.**

126 **I've changed my bank password to 'incorrect', now if I forget it reminds me 'your password is incorrect'.........how good is that?**

127 **On a first date I tend to ask about the street she grew up in, her first pets, birthday, that sort of thing....at least then if I don't get anywhere I'll have access to her passwords.**

128 **I've got a new app for my mobile phone. It's a phone box locator!**

129 **Yesterday the man died who invented predictive text. His funfair is next monkey.**

130 **I went online and bought a DVD on 'How to handle disappointment'. When I opened it, it was empty.**

131 **Hey kids, try the new social media networking tool ...it's called 'outside'.**

132 **You can't always find exactly what you want on the Internet. I searched for cigarette lighters and got 10,000 matches.**

133 **Ironic....someone on Facebook saying 'get a life'.**

134 **Maybe if we tell the teenagers their brain is an app they will start using it.**

Knock Knock

135 **Knock knock. Who's there? It's me, Grandpa..... wait, stop the funeral!**

136 **Knock knock. Who's there? Dyslexia. Dyslexia how?**

Magician

137 **I was driving along and I smashed into a magician. It wasn't my fault, he came out of nowhere.**

138 **It's funny when a magician needs to sneeze, he can't get his hanky out quick enough because it's always 3 feet long.**

Medical

139 **My boyfriend says the doctor wanted a urine sample, and faeces sample. I told him, "Just hand over your boxer shorts."**

140 **A man walks into a psychiatrist's wearing only cling film for shorts. The psychiatrist says, "Well I can clearly see you're nuts."**

141 **I said to the pharmacist, "If I ask you for Viagra will I be able to get it over the counter?" She said, "You will if you take two!"**

Men

142 **If a man says he'll fix something there's no need to remind him every six months.**

143 **My husband and I divorced over religious differences. He thought he was God and I didn't.**

Misc.

144 **I don't do many innuendos but I do slip one in occasionally.**

145 **How many optometrists does it take to change a light bulb? ......one or two..........one or two.......**

146 **I used to work for the Samaritans, but every time you call in sick they try to talk you out of it.**

147 **I phoned the incontinence hotline last night..... and all you get is a voice saying, "Can you hold please?"**

148 **A dog walker was found dead in the local park; the police have found the dog but they haven't got a lead.**

149 **I had to take the batteries out of my carbon monoxide detector; the constant beeping was making me nauseous.**

150 **I was at the ice cream van. I said, "I want to buy an ice cream please". He said, "Hundreds and thousands." I said, "We'll start with one and see how we go."**

151 **Bloke was found on the floor of his ice cream van covered in nuts and sprinkles........police think he topped himself.**

152 **It's the anniversary today of when the boomerang was invented........many happy returns.**

153 **I'm really annoyed. The local Neighbourhood Watch group had a meeting last night about some creepy weirdo in the area and I wasn't invited.**

154 **Police called at the house and said, "We have reason to believe that on August 15th you skateboarded down Kenilworth high street, naked, with a firework up your backside singing The Laughing Policeman. What do you have to say?" I said, "What was that date again?"**

155 **A guy knocked on my door and asked for a donation towards the new local swimming pool. I gave him a glass of water.**

156 **An Englishman, Scotsman and Irishman go into a pub...... the landlord says, "Is this some kind of joke?"**

157 **My mate keeps drinking brake fluid, but he says he's not addicted......he can stop when he wants.**

158 **A woman walks into a bar and asks for a 'double entendre' ....so the barman gives her one.**

159 **My blinking neighbour was banging on my door at 3 o'clock this morning....lucky I was still up playing the drums.**

160 **My mate had an accident and fell in an upholstery machine, but fortunately he's completely recovered.**

161 **I've just been done for my part in a timeshare fraud, luckily I only have to go to prison two weeks every year.**

162 **A girl lying in the sun on a park bench. A tramp says, "eh luv, what about the two of us getting it on?" Horrified she says, "What sort of girl do you think I am? I'm not one of your cheap pick-ups." The tramp says, "Well you're already lying in my bed."**

163 **Two parrots sitting on a perch, one says to the other, "Can you smell fish?"**

164 **I ordered some bubble wrap just to see what it got delivered in.**

165 **I went on a website about toasters but there were too many pop-ups.**

166 **I went up to this guy selling The Big Issue the other day. I said, "Knock, knock", he said, "Who's there?" I said, "I thought you were supposed to be homeless?"**

167 **I got sacked from my job in the Salvation Army soup kitchen- all I said was, "Hurry up you lot, some of us have got homes to go to!"**

168 **My friend's wife left him last week. He said she was going out for a bottle of milk and never came back. I said, "How are you coping?" "Not too bad" he said, "I'm getting by on the powdered stuff."**

169 **I saw a billboard poster saying "Learn to read". I thought, who are they aiming that poster at?**

170 **A man has been jailed for assaulting a fortune teller who predicted he would go to jail.**

171 **I saw Sky News showing the riots in Greece, the whole place looks like it's in ruins.**

172 **I saw a sign on the maternity room door. It said, 'Push, push, push.'**

173 **I bought a brand new boomerang, but I don't seem to be able to throw the old one away.**

174 **A container ship full of blue paint has collided into a ship full of red paint. The crew have been marooned.**

175 **Remember boys and girls, do not handle any fireworks, leave it to the adults who have been drinking all day.**

176 **I lost my pet mouse 'Elvis' yesterday....he was 'caught in a trap' and couldn't get out.**

177 **Why can't life's problems hit us when we are 18 and know everything?**

178 **I've just bought a pair of binoculars, really pricey, £900. I reckon the guy saw me coming.**

179 **The trouble with the girls in our house is that they always forget to leave the toilet seat up.**

180 **I tried to get rid of my old boomerang by throwing it really, really hard.......now I live in constant fear.**

181 **What do diarrhoea and electric cars have in common? ....Will I make it home?**

182 **We've had a letter from Bill Bailey.......he's decided to come home.**

183 **I don't drink, don't smoke, don't womanise all night; but things will change when I get out of prison.**

184 **I was gonna tell a joke about time-travelling. But you guys didn't like it.**

185 **Why can't your hand be 12 inches long? Because then it'd be a foot.**

186 **Some days I have to take three or four baths to make the phone ring.**

187 **What was the best thing before they invented sliced bread?**

188 **Bloke at an auction bought a parrot. He says to the auctioneer, "I paid an awful lot of money for this parrot but I never even checked if it could talk." The auctioneer responded, " I wouldn't worry too much about that Sir.....who do you think was bidding against you?"**

189 **A woman on trial for beating him over the head with his guitar collection. The Judge asks, "First offender?" She says, "No, first a Gibson, then a Fender".**

190 **The most common lie from a Welshman is, "I was only trying to help that sheep over the fence."**

191 **The boss of Ryanair walks into a bar thinking Guinness at £2 pint is cheap. The barman smiles and says, "Would you like a glass with that?"**

192 **Shoplifting from an Apple store strictly speaking should just count as scrumping.**

193 **I used to sell Filofaxes to the mafia; I was involved in very organised crime.**

194 **The main difference between Dubai and Abu Dhabi is that people in Dubai don't like The Flintstones, but people in Abu Dhabidoooo.**

195 **Some woman described me the other day as 'A bit of a looker'. Well I say that........creepy voyeur were her actual words.**

196 **Why is it called Alcoholics Anonymous when the first thing you do is stand up and say, "I'm an alcoholic and my name's Simon"?**

197 **No matter how nice the soap smells, never leave a public toilet sniffing your fingers.**

198 **I sat in the pub with the missus, I looked at these two old buggers, I said, "That's us in ten years"...she said, "That's a mirror!"**

199 **Why do frisbees get larger the closer they get?.....then it hit me.**

200 **My mate was run over by a steam roller. The nurse said he's in ward 15,16 and 17.**

201 **Incredible to think every Scotsman started out as a scotch egg!**

202 **I've got a stalker...everywhere I go she's there 10 paces in front of me.**

203 **At Alton Towers it's always fun to bring a few nuts and bolts out of your pocket and show them to the person sitting next to you once the ride has begun.**

204 **A chicken walks up to a duck who is about to cross the road. He says, "Don't do it mate you'll never hear the end of it."**

205 **Anne Robinson's left the Weakest Link but her surgeon has put a brave face on her........**

206 **I wonder what "Don't touch" is in Braille.**

207 **Did you hear about the ship carrying a consignment of yo-yos? .....It sank thirty-four times.**

208 **My grandad was famous for inventing the first door knocker......he was awarded the Nobel Prize.**

209 **Every time I hear of someone being attacked by a shark I think "Didn't they hear the music?"**

210 **I don't know what's best about Switzerland, but of course the flag's a big plus.**

211 **I bought a leopard skin coat off Amazon......it was spotless when it arrived so I sent it back.**

212 **These paperless offices are OK but what do you do when you go to the toilet?**

213 **If you don't want to go on holiday you can get the same effect by staying at home and tipping every second person you see.**

214 **I've got a new stopwatch ....0-60 in one minute.**

215 **A Royal Engineer serving overseas wrote 200 letters a month to his girlfriend back home. This Saturday at All Saints Church she marries the postman.**

216 **I wondered "Do prostitutes have babies?" .... of course they do, where do you think traffic wardens come from?**

217 **Why do we all feel safe under the blankets? It's not like a murderer will come in thinking, "I'm gonna kill....oh damn he's under a blanket."**

218 **I've put an electric fence around my back garden.....the neighbour's dead against it.**

219 **I said to this beautiful girl, "Hey gorgeous where have you been all my life?" She said, "For the first half of it I wasn't even alive!"**

220 **I don't mind people telling me they're gay, I just don't want them ramming it down my throat.**

221 **Talk about luck. A bloke wins £120 million on the lottery and two days later meets the love of his life.**

222 **How much does a grand piano cost? About £1000. (a Grand!)**

223 **An odd thing happened to me yesterday. I found a hat with some money in it. Next thing you know a bloke with a guitar is chasing me down the road.**

224 **Did you hear about the statistician who drowned while crossing a river? It was three feet deep on average.**

225 **My next door neighbour has a green triangular house. My other next door neighbour has a yellow rectangular house. And the people across the road have an orange octagonal house... I live in a quality street.**

226 **Who was the first man to sail around the world single handed? Robin Knox Johnson? Sir Francis Chichester? ..... no.... Captain Hook!**

227 **The world champion tongue twister got arrested. I hear they're going to give him a tough sentence.**

228 **The man who invented Velcro has died........R.I.P.**

229 **The only benefit from studying algebra is that it helped us when our children needed help with their algebra.**

230 **I made the house completely childproof......... but they're still getting in.**

231 **My son's always on his Playstation. I said, "Why don't you go outside for a while?" "It's raining," he grunted. I said, "Well it's your lucky day, they've just discovered that skin is waterproof!"**

Mother-in-law

232 **I knew her mother was coming round when I saw the canary throw itself in the cat's mouth.**

233 **The mother-in-law came round unexpectedly yesterday..............that's the last time I buy cheap chloroform.**

Motoring

234 **Dead car batteries......don't get me started.**

235 **Just bought Pavarotti's old car....it's a Nissan Dorma.**

236 **Yesterday I had to put air in my tyres. It was a pound to use the machine. I remember when it was 10p. That's inflation for you.**

237 **Driverless cars......they're just around the corner.**

238 **Have you ever noticed that anyone going slower than you is an idiot, and anyone going faster is a maniac?**

239 **I love sat nav ...don't know where I'd be without it.**

Music

240 **I still remember that Beatles song like it was yesterday.**

241 **Does anyone in the room know a Delilah? Or is it just Tom Jones?**

242 **I got a guitar delivered yesterday but it was addressed to someone else. I just wrote on the box, 'Return to Fender'.**

243 **I said, Doctor I keep singing 'The Green, Green, Grass of Home'. He said, "You've got Tom Jones Syndrome". I said, "Is it common?" He replied "It's not unusual."**

Politics	244	**Apparently the Houses of Parliament are infected with vermin......at least that's what the rats are saying.**
Sex	245	**I went to bed with a blind girl last night, she said I had the biggest whatsit she'd ever laid her hands on .... I said, "You're pulling my leg."**
	246	**To spice things up in the bedroom I went on Amazon and bought '101 Mating Positions'. My sex life's still crap but my chess has improved.**
	247	**I'd like to have a sex change....from none to absolutely loads.**
	248	**I read that men who make love 4 times a week live on average 12 years longer than men who don't. I said to the wife, "You're trying to kill me." She said, "No, it sounds like you're trying to kill me."**
	249	**I think I must be in a 'same sex relationship'........put it another way, after 20 years the sex is just the same.**
	250	**My lesbian neighbours gave me a Rolex; I think they misunderstood me when I said, I wanna watch!**

251 **I'm a sex object.......I suggest sex and she objects.**

252 **Always read the instructions on the Viagra box and never take more that the recommended dose; trust me I found out the hard way.**

253 **Oysters are supposed to be good aphrodisiacs? I tried a dozen but only 3 of them worked.**

254 **Don't be frightened of trying a bit of bondage........maybe get someone to show you the ropes.**

255 **If I come across any innuendo, I'll whip it out immediately.**

256 **Two men discussing sex. One says to the other, "Are you a 'oncer' or a 'twicer' "? "A 'twicer'," says the other guy. "Which do you prefer?" says the first man........ "Oh I think the winter one!" says the other bloke.**

257 **I got myself fitted with a pacemaker. Now every time I have sex with the missus, the garage door opens.**

Sleep

258 **I won't rest until I find a cure for insomnia.**

259 **I slept through the alarm this morning, luckily it was only a small fire.**

260 **I bought some sleeping tablets. The label said, 'Warning. May cause drowsiness'.**

Sport

261 **Deep down, I knew that scuba diving wasn't for me.**

262 **After 5 karate lessons I can now break a two-inch thick bread board with my plaster cast.**

263 **The trouble with jogging is that by the time you realise you're not in shape for it, it's too far to walk back.**

264 **I went to the ballet once; I couldn't even tell who won.**

265 **You get these mountain climbers roping themselves together. It's in case one comes to his senses and wants to go home.**

266 **There has never been a fisherman who could keep both hands in his pockets when describing the one that got away.**

Stress

267 **I read an article which says typical signs of stress are, eating too much, impulse buying and driving too fast ....my idea of a perfect day!**

Super-market

268 **Two tigers walking down the aisle of a supermarket. One says to the other, "Do you think it's quiet in here today?"**

269 **The staff at our supermarket are so slow I started using the self check-out service ....I was named 'employee of the month'.**

270 **If you ever feel the world is moving too fast, take comfort from the queue at the supermarket checkout.**

271 **If ASDA lower prices every day why isn't anything in the shop free yet?**

272 **I love a bargain....... we've got a back garden full of shopping trolleys.....they're only a pound each.**

273 **How can you spot the people who can't count to 10? They are the ones in front of you in the fast check-out lane.**

Tennis

274 **I said to my son will you please stop watching porn, your mother and me can hear it in the next room. He said, "Dad it's Maria Sharapova at Wimbledon."**

275 **Andy Murray went into the library and asks for a couple of books on great tennis serves. The librarian says, "No, you'll never return them."**

276 **Tennis....all that grunting, we turn it up so the neighbours think we're having sex.**

Train 277 **The train was ever so busy; even all the men couldn't get seats.**

278 **I came here on a train tonight......passenger announcement: "This is a passenger announcement, the train that has just arrived at platform 1,2,3,4 &5 has come in sideways."**

Vegetarian 279 **What would you do if you saw an endangered animal eating an endangered plant?**

Weather 280 **People always complain about the weather but nobody does anything about it.**

Weather 281 **Beastly weather occurs when it rains cats and dogs.**

Wife 282 **The wife's bisexual......what I really mean is she only does it twice a year.**

283 **To liven things up I've changed the bed for a trampoline .....last night the wife hit the roof.**

284 **The wife says to spice things up let's each pick a fantasy partner.....you know..... she says, "Mine's George Clooney, who's yours?" .....Well, when I said, 'The babysitter' all hell broke loose.**

285 **The wife says, "You never tell me how much you love me." I said, "I know, I don't want to upset you."**

286 **The wife swallowed a load of scrabble tiles; she's in hospital because the doctor says if she goes to the toilet it could spell disaster.**

287 **When I met the wife she said she didn't believe in sex before marriage...I should have checked she believed in it after marriage.**

288 **My wife and I have an agreement. She does what she wants and I do what she wants.**

289 **I always know when the wife's up...... I can hear her scraping the toast.**

290 **I tried that internet dating, but I soon realised it wasn't for me when they matched me up with the wife.**

291 **The wife was really flattered when they named a rose after her, mind you she wasn't too pleased when she read the description in the catalogue....'not much good in a bed, but fine up against a wall'.**

292 **I said to the wife "I'll try not to be condescending; that means I won't talk down to you."**

293 **The wife said, "If you were half a man you would take the kids to the circus." I said, "If I was half a man, I'd be in the circus."** (MICK MILLER)

294 **The wife's got a new job, but it's not easy to say what it is.....she sells seashells on the sea shore.**

295 **I bought the wife a new fridge for her birthday. She wasn't pleased....... but her face lit up when she opened the door.**

296 **Wife came home, just back from the beauty parlour. I said, "What's wrong, was it closed?"**

297 **I say to the wife I love you just the way you are, but she never listens, she just goes on putting weight on.**

298 **The wife said, "Will you stop walking round the house singing I'm a believer". I didn't know what she was on about....then I saw her face.**

299 **The wife came home and caught me wearing her best dress....I said, "Don't leave me, I can change."**

300 **The wife left me, she says I think more about football than her....I was gutted, I've been with that girl for 5 seasons.**

301 **My wife gave me a book on Feng Shui.......I didn't know where to put it.**

302 **I bought my wife a rug off eBay. It said mint condition. When I got it, there was a hole in the middle.**

303 **My wife says every time our neighbour sees his wife he kisses her. "Why can't you do that?" I said, "I hardly know her."**

304 **I said to my wife "Do you really need to iron that bra, there's not that much to put in it?" She replied, "I iron your boxer shorts don't I?"**

305 **The wife was feeling unwell so I phoned the doctor for advice. He said, "Is she hot?" I said, "Well with a little make-up, and a short skirt...."**

306 **She says I'm full of my own importance..... anyway that's enough about her...**

307 **The wife said she keeps getting emails offering her cans of processed meat. I said, "It's only spam."**

308 **Me and the wife always hold hands. Well I say that......... if I let her go, she goes shopping.**

309 **I was shopping with the wife the other day. She went into a dress shop so I popped into the bookies just to kill a bit of time. A bloke comes up to me and says, "Do you want the winner of the 4.30 at Uttoxeter?" I said, "To be honest mate I've only got a small back garden."**

310 **Why did my wife cross the road? To go back into the first shoe shop we went in 3 hours ago.**

311 **The wife dated a clown before we met....so I had some pretty big shoes to fill.**

312 **The wife comes from a long line of conga dancers.**

313 **I should have known it was a mistake to get married....after I said, "I do", the vicar looked at her then turned to me and said, "Is that your final answer?"**

314 **I told the wife she'd drawn her eyebrows on too high...she looked surprised.**

315 **Every night the wife puts that mudpack on her face and slices of cucumber on her eyes. It doesn't work though, I can still tell it's her.**

316 **The wife sent me shopping today. She said, "Buy something to make me look sexy."....so I came back with a two-litre bottle of vodka.**

317 **It was the wife's birthday so I went into Ann Summers and said, "Have you got a see-through nighty please?" She said, "What size?" I said, "58-49-65." She said, "Are you sure you want to see through to that?"**

318 **My wife used to have a hourglass figure....but the sands of time have shifted a bit....I said to her, "You've put on a lot of weight." "No I haven't", she said. I thought, 'I'm gonna win this one'......I said, "You used to be 7lb 4 oz."**

319 **The wife said she wanted something that does 0-60 in 5 seconds for Christmas, hint, hint......... I've bought her a set of bathroom scales.**

320 **The wife says I ruined her birthday...... I said, "Don't be so absurd, I didn't even know it was your birthday."**

321 **The wife's been really helpful to me, otherwise I would have thought I had no faults.**

322 **I've just been given two weeks to live......why are you smiling?......well, what I mean is the wife's going away to her sister's for two weeks.**

323 **My missus is a stunner.........well I say that; she's got a new job down at the abattoir.**

324 **The wife said, "Simmo you're rubbish in bed", so as a special surprise for her, two very nice girls have been helping me train to improve......**

325 **The wife said she suspected me of being a transvestite......so I packed her things and left.**

326 **The wife's on a diet of coconuts and bananas......she hasn't lost any weight but she can't half climb trees.**

327 **My wife texted me after a row to say I was very condescending. To be honest I was surprised she even could spell it.**

328 **The wife says I'm nosey and intrusive.....at least that's what it says in her diary.**

329 **My wife's from Scotland, she loves summer. It used to be her favourite day of the year.**

330 **The wife spent two hours at the beautician's yesterday, they didn't actually do anything, they were just preparing the estimate.**

331 **The wife's threatening to leave me because apparently I'm a smart arse. She says the relationship is at a crossroads. One way is love and trust, the other is divorce. I said, "I think you'll find that is a T junction not a crossroads!"**

332 **I said to the wife, "There's a burglar downstairs in the kitchen eating that pie you made this afternoon." She said, "Ring 999." I said, "Shall I ask for the Police or an Ambulance?"**

333 **The wife went to the doctor with 'ladies things', she says he told her she needs to have sex 5 times a week........ I said, "Put me down for Mondays and Fridays."**

334 **I said to the wife, "It isn't your jeans that make your bum look fat."**

335 **The wife says I never listen to what she says.... or something like that.**

336 **My wife said, "Will you still love me when I'm old and ugly?" I said, "Of course I do."**

337 **I said to the wife, "Fancy a quicky?" She responded, "As opposed to what?"**

338 **My wife left me because of my terrible gambling habit....... But I'm looking at ways of winning her back.**

339 **My wife's leaving me because of my obsession with rugby. I keep pleading with her to give it one more try.**

340 **My wife told me to stop impersonating a flamingo. I had to put my foot down.**

341 **The wife has always been so angry with me that she turned round the first time I whistled.**

342 **The missus is always wanting to keep up with the Joneses: we've got a big square patio so she's had me paint it blue so all the people looking on Google Earth think we've got a swimming pool.**

343 **I said to the missus, "Were you faking it last night?" She said, "No, I really was asleep."**

344 **The wife said, "What would you call me if I said I was having sex with your best friend?" The husband replied, "A lesbian".**

345 **I said to the wife, "Shall we go on a world cruise?" She replied, "Can't we go somewhere else?"**

346 **The wife's putting her foot down and says that's it, choose me or football. I said, "Give me 90 minutes to think about it!"**

Women

347 **You don't appreciate a lot of stuff in school until you get older. Little things like being spanked by a middle-aged woman everyday....... things you'd pay good money for in later life.**

348 **Why is it so hard for women to find men that are sensitive, caring and attractive? Those men already have boyfriends.**

349 **A study has shown that women who carry a little weight tend to live longer than men who mention it.**

350 **After years of trying to figure women out, I'm moving on to much simpler subjects - like quantum physics.**

351 **She said she was approaching 40, but I couldn't help wondering from which direction?**

352 **Well girls, when you're lying on the beach wearing a bikini, the worst thing you can hear is "good for you".**

353 **Last night my girlfriend was complaining that I never listen to her... or something like that.**

354 **She maybe an heiress, but she looks more like an heirloom.**

Work

355 **A friend of ours has just lost his job as an archaeologist......to be honest his job was in ruins anyway.**

356 **I was very big in the cement business; I was a great mixer.**

357 **I got a new job as a waiter, the pay's rubbish but at least it puts food on the table.**

358 **The boss said to me, "In a rare moment I'm going to mix business with pleasure - you're fired."**

359 **I wanted to be a barber....but I just couldn't cut it.**

360 **I once had a job interview to be a mustard cutter ....but I wasn't quite up to it.**

361 **My mate on the dodgems has lost his job. He's suing for 'funfair dismissal'!**

362 **Most people are shocked when they find out how bad I am as an electrician.**

363 **A friend of mine owned a balloon company, but sadly he had to close it. Couldn't keep up with the cost of inflation.**

364 **I have a few jokes about unemployed people, but none of them work.**

365 **I've been thinking about my career. Upon reflection, I could see myself working in a mirror factory. (*Two jokes in one!)***

And there's more……

Magic Tricks

As well as a little stand up comedy, 'The Great Simmoni' has a reputation for crazy magic tricks.
Scan the following QR codes to join the fun……

1

A mixed comedy magic act with Mentalism and then a disappearing bottle of orange.

SCAN ME

2

Levitation with a magic comedy twist ?

SCAN ME

3

Sawing a woman in half. This act uses a real electric jigsaw with an extended blade. I was very nervous on the night and lost many nights sleep wondering if it could go wrong.....

SCAN ME

4

Escapology, Transformation, Levitation and murder Mystery thrown in. A complex crazy routine. The 'Magicians Assistant' transforms to become a different girl.....

SCAN ME

5

Amateur comic magic tricks. Dippy the Duck features well, with some hand chopping to finish the show.

SCAN ME

I would send a huge thank you to my graphic artist
and book designer Elizabeth Heissler.
I feel her ideas have been fantastic and she has endless
patience when it comes to revisions and edits.
Thanks go to my son Iain for proof reading over
and over again. We've all had a load of fun
working on the Richard Simmons
vanity project!

Notes

Notes